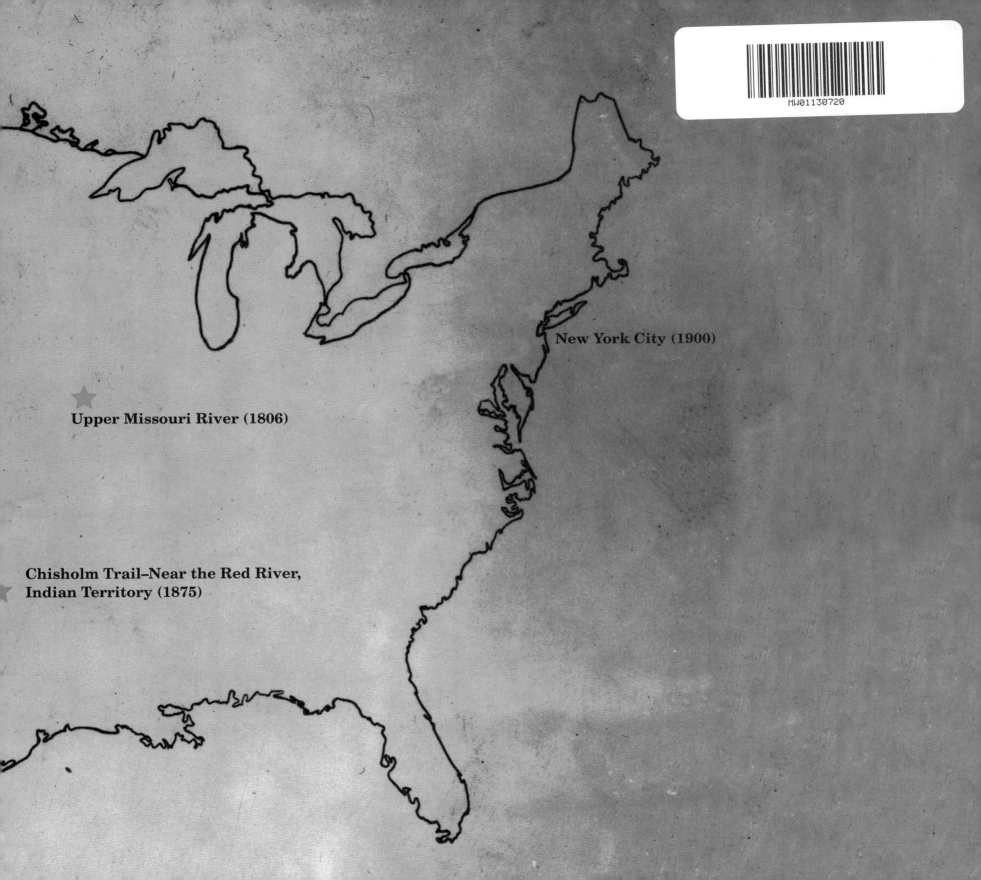

New York City (1900)

Upper Missouri River (1806)

Chisholm Trail–Near the Red River,
Indian Territory (1875)

VOICES of the WESTERN FRONTIER

Sherry Garland

Illustrated by Julie Dupré Buckner

PELICAN PUBLISHING COMPANY
GRETNA 2016

The word "Pelican" and the depiction of a pelican are trademarks of Pelican Publishing Company, Inc., and are registered in the U.S. Patent and Trademark Office.

Library of Congress Cataloging-in-Publication Data

Names: Garland, Sherry. | Buckner, Julie Dupré, illustrator.
Title: Voices of the western frontier / by Sherry Garland ; illustrated by
   Julie Dupré Buckner.
Description: Gretna : Pelican Publishing Company, 2016. | Includes
   bibliographical references.
Identifiers: LCCN 2015025889| ISBN 9781455619610 (hardcover : alk.
paper) |
   ISBN 9781455619627 (e-book)
Subjects: LCSH: Frontier and pioneer life—West (U.S.)—Juvenile
literature.
   | West (U.S.)—Social life and customs—Juvenile literature.
Classification: LCC F596 .G36 2016 | DDC 978—dc23 LC record
available at http://lccn.loc.gov/2015025889

Printed in Malaysia
Published by Pelican Publishing Company, Inc.
1000 Burmaster Street, Gretna, Louisiana 70053

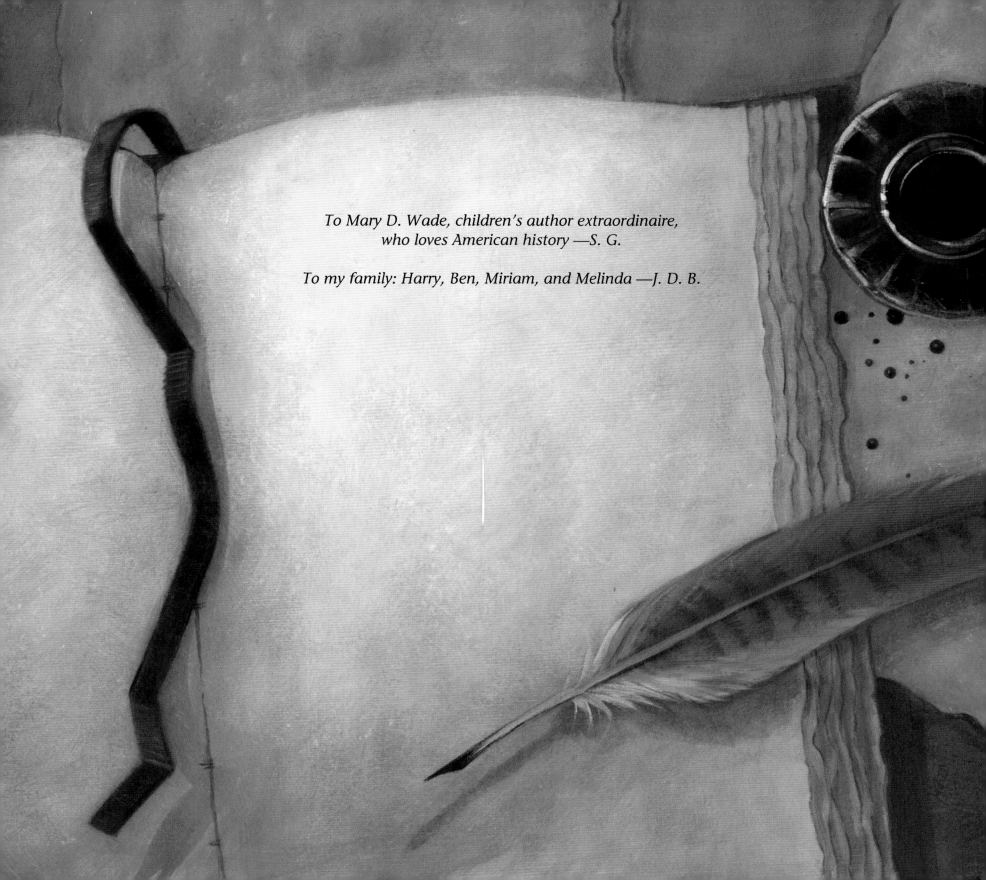

*To Mary D. Wade, children's author extraordinaire,
who loves American history —S. G.*

To my family: Harry, Ben, Miriam, and Melinda —J. D. B.

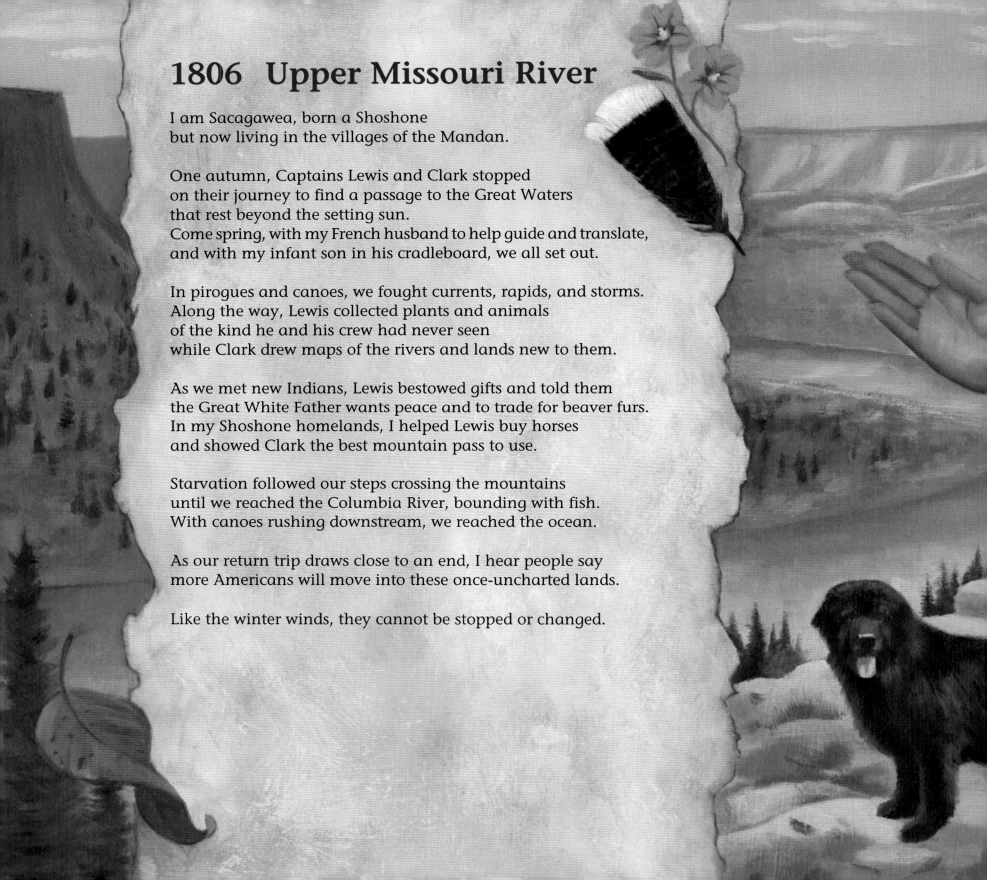

1806 Upper Missouri River

I am Sacagawea, born a Shoshone
but now living in the villages of the Mandan.

One autumn, Captains Lewis and Clark stopped
on their journey to find a passage to the Great Waters
that rest beyond the setting sun.
Come spring, with my French husband to help guide and translate,
and with my infant son in his cradleboard, we all set out.

In pirogues and canoes, we fought currents, rapids, and storms.
Along the way, Lewis collected plants and animals
of the kind he and his crew had never seen
while Clark drew maps of the rivers and lands new to them.

As we met new Indians, Lewis bestowed gifts and told them
the Great White Father wants peace and to trade for beaver furs.
In my Shoshone homelands, I helped Lewis buy horses
and showed Clark the best mountain pass to use.

Starvation followed our steps crossing the mountains
until we reached the Columbia River, bounding with fish.
With canoes rushing downstream, we reached the ocean.

As our return trip draws close to an end, I hear people say
more Americans will move into these once-uncharted lands.

Like the winter winds, they cannot be stopped or changed.

1825   Rocky Mountains, at the Green River

I am Jedediah Smith, a mountain man
trapping beaver in these cold rivers and streams.

I polished my hunting skills and
learned Indian ways to survive.
In the winter I trap the furry animals
while in the summer I sell the pelts
and replenish my supplies.

The dangers are many—freezing cold,
rugged mountains, and dreaded grizzly bears
like the one that left scars down my face.
My most-prized possessions are my Bible
and the *Journals of Lewis and Clark.*

Since the Louisiana Purchase twenty-two years ago,
trappers have been depleting the beaver everywhere.

Surely those bucky-tooth critters will soon be gone
from this land of beauty and majesty—
what then will gentlemen do for their fancy beaver hats?

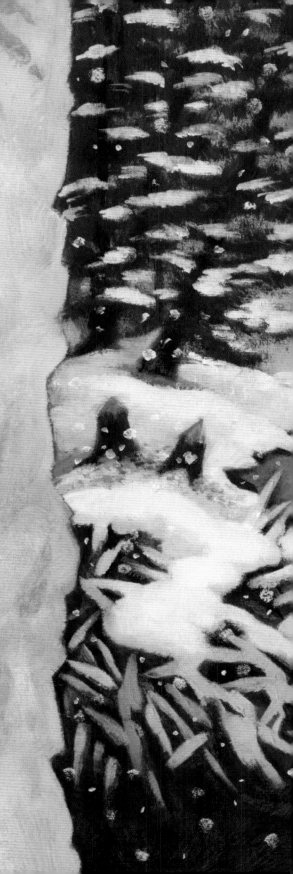

1835 Black Hills

I am George Catlin, painter and author,
traversing mountains, hills, and plains
to preserve on canvas the manners and customs
of the North American Indians living here.

Today I am in the land of the Lakota Sioux
in this month called "moon of falling leaves"
trying to sketch the thrill of the bison hunt
as Indians ride their horses dangerously close
to the massive herd, lance and bow in hand.
With lightning speed and unparalleled skill,
they surround a *tatanka* and bring it to its knees.

The women will help skin and butcher the animals,
then cook or dry the meat back at the tipis not far away.
The bison is sacred to them: every part is used
for food, tools, weapons, clothing, or shelter coverings.

The people have been honest, hospitable, and faithful.
As long as I can, I will try to capture the dignity
of these worthy people in this breathtaking land.

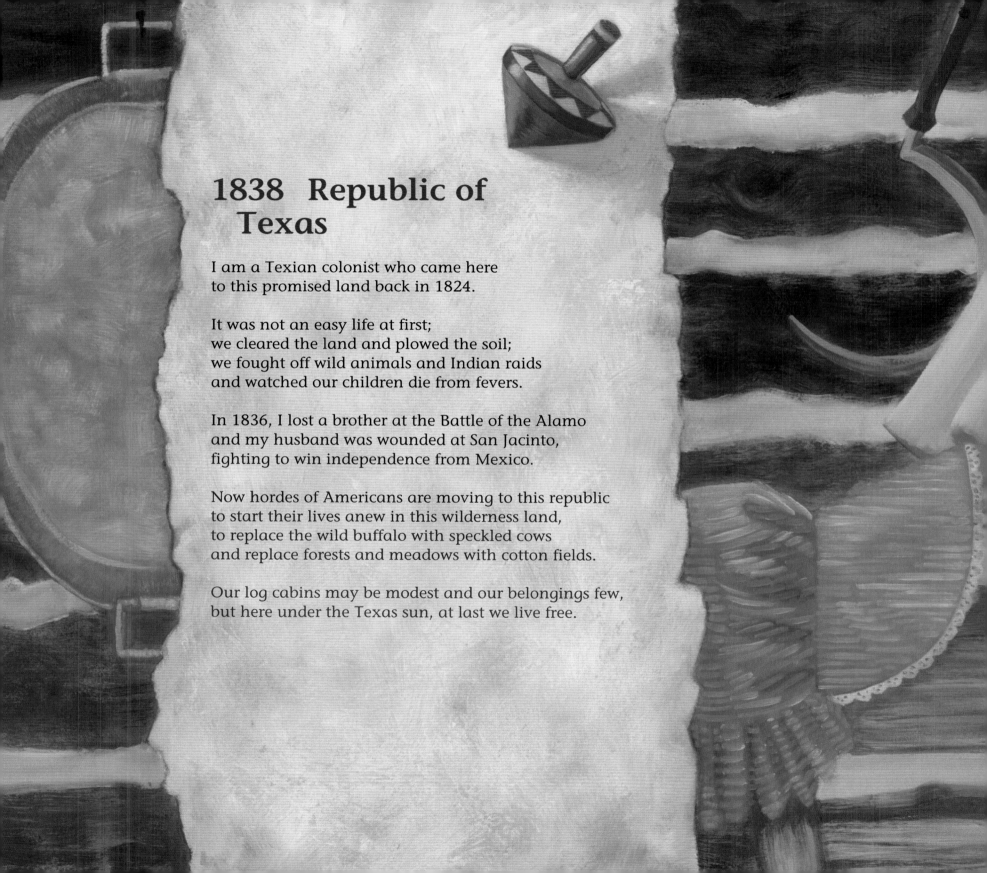

1838 Republic of Texas

I am a Texian colonist who came here
to this promised land back in 1824.

It was not an easy life at first;
we cleared the land and plowed the soil;
we fought off wild animals and Indian raids
and watched our children die from fevers.

In 1836, I lost a brother at the Battle of the Alamo
and my husband was wounded at San Jacinto,
fighting to win independence from Mexico.

Now hordes of Americans are moving to this republic
to start their lives anew in this wilderness land,
to replace the wild buffalo with speckled cows
and replace forests and meadows with cotton fields.

Our log cabins may be modest and our belongings few,
but here under the Texas sun, at last we live free.

1846   Near the Platte River

I am a girl walking along the Oregon Trail
beside my family's prairie schooner.

It is packed with everything we'll need
for the six-month trip across the West.
Papa's farming tools are in there, too,
for starting over where the soil is fertile.

At sunrise the wagons leave, rocking and jostling
over the rough ground, kicking up dust or mud.
Every day we see items tossed aside to lighten loads—
pianos, tables, chairs—wish I could take them all.

At river crossings, the cows and horses can swim
but wagons use ferries or float across on their bases.

Come evening time, we pitch the tents for the night
and cook supper with a fire made from buffalo chips
collected by my brothers and me along the way.

Another day and we have traveled fifteen miles;
another day closer to Oregon and our dreams.

1848 Santa Fe,
New Mexico Area

I am a white-bearded merchant whose ancestors
came here from Spain many generations ago.
I own a bustling trading post on the Santa Fe Trail.

Mexican traders bring silver coins, wool, and mules;
trappers from the Rockies bring furs and hides;
American traders coming from Missouri, 900 miles away,
bring manufactured goods like weapons and tools.
And for the ladies—calico, needles, and thread.

When mule trains arrive, covered in dust,
such a noisy din you've never heard!

But during the past two years the United States
and Mexico were fighting a war, a futile thing.
Now Mexico is forced to sell to the United States
all her lands from Texas to sunny California.

No doubt, even more Americans will be moving out West,
but I don't mind: that means more trade for me.

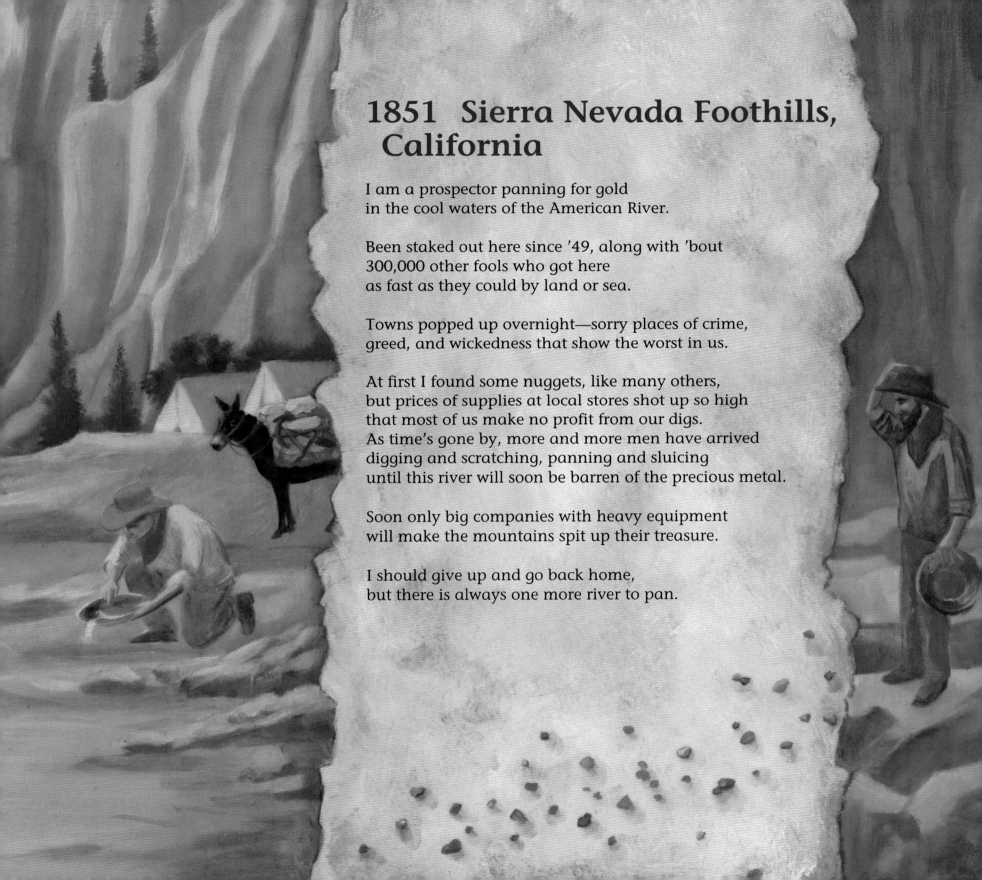

1851 Sierra Nevada Foothills, California

I am a prospector panning for gold
in the cool waters of the American River.

Been staked out here since '49, along with 'bout
300,000 other fools who got here
as fast as they could by land or sea.

Towns popped up overnight—sorry places of crime,
greed, and wickedness that show the worst in us.

At first I found some nuggets, like many others,
but prices of supplies at local stores shot up so high
that most of us make no profit from our digs.
As time's gone by, more and more men have arrived
digging and scratching, panning and sluicing
until this river will soon be barren of the precious metal.

Soon only big companies with heavy equipment
will make the mountains spit up their treasure.

I should give up and go back home,
but there is always one more river to pan.

1861 Nevada Territory

I am a rider for the Pony Express.
Been in the saddle more than ten hours,
rising and falling, rising and falling,
trying not to think about my aching bones.

I'm a little runt—the kind of kid the company wants
to ride the swift Indian ponies at a gallop
on this leg of the route from Missouri to California—
1,900 miles in only ten days guaranteed!

At each relay station, 'bout twenty miles apart,
I grab the leather mail pouch from the saddle,
jump off the worn-out horse, and leap onto a fresh one.
Then it's off like the wind we go again!

I see an Overland Stagecoach ahead
swinging and swaying, carrying passengers and mail.
Men stretch their necks, waving hats out the windows,
and women wave their dainty handkerchiefs at me.
No time to stop; I just give them a nod and ride on.

I will be nothing but a black speck to them soon enough;
then it's just me, my thoughts, and the pounding hooves.

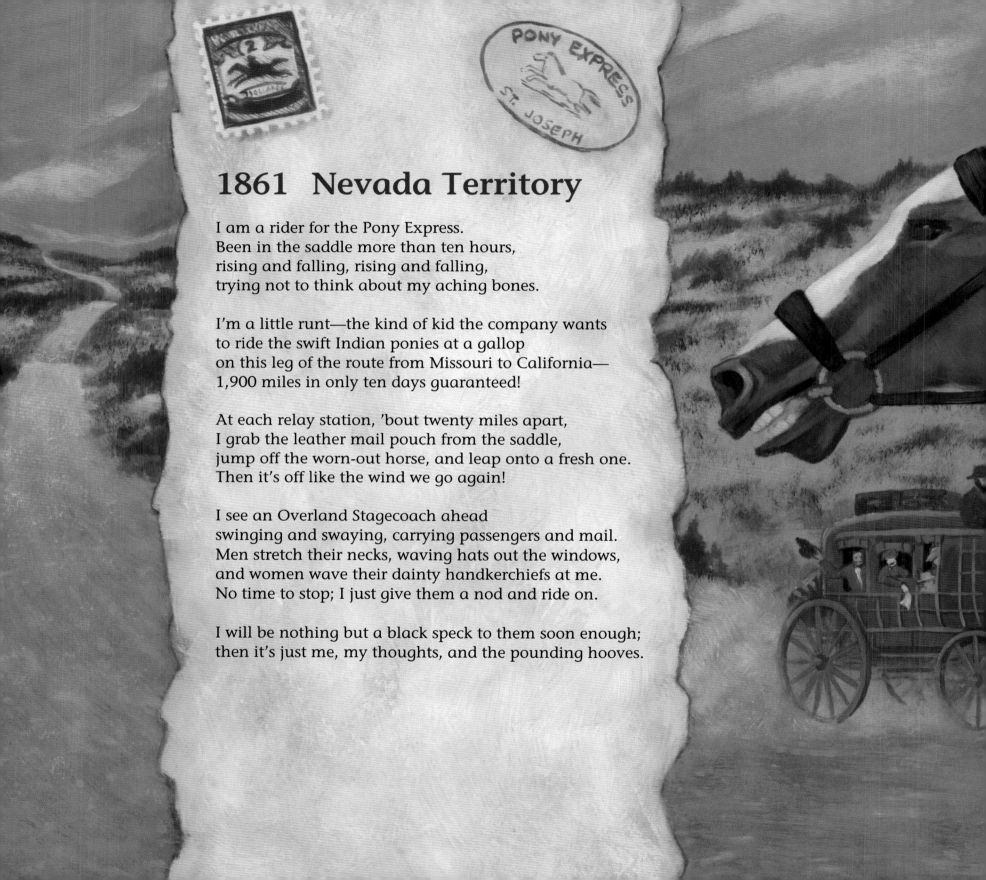

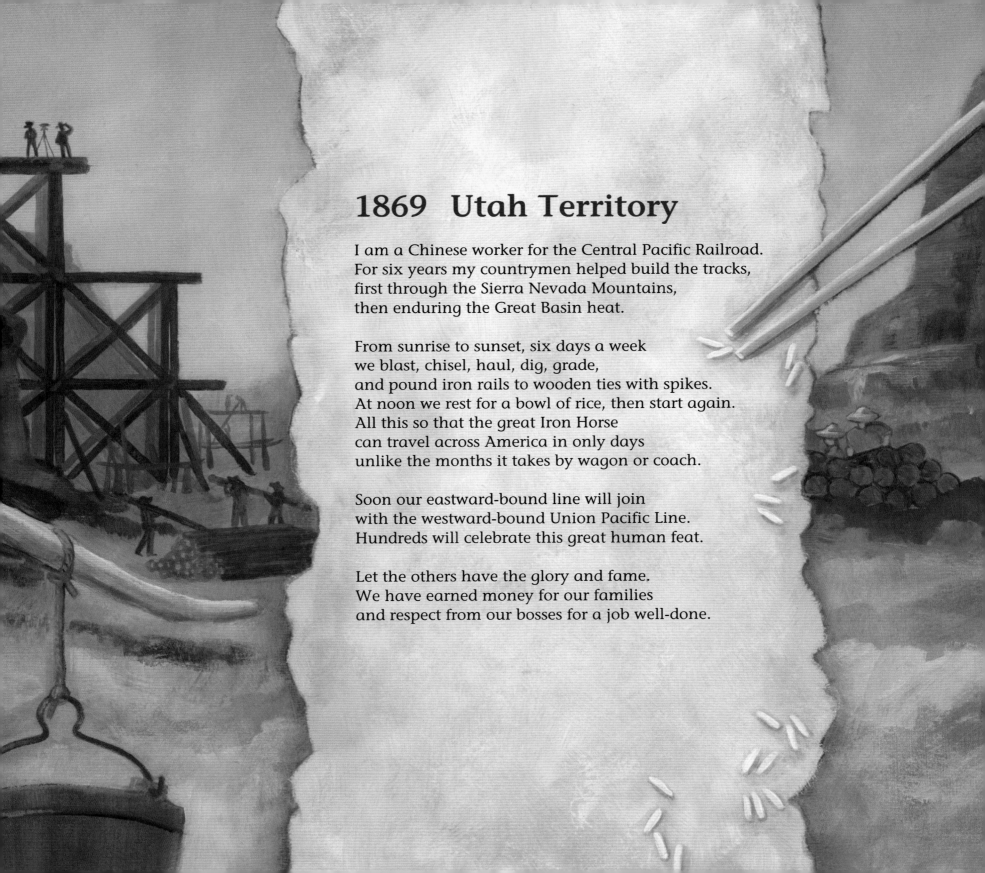

1869 Utah Territory

I am a Chinese worker for the Central Pacific Railroad.
For six years my countrymen helped build the tracks,
first through the Sierra Nevada Mountains,
then enduring the Great Basin heat.

From sunrise to sunset, six days a week
we blast, chisel, haul, dig, grade,
and pound iron rails to wooden ties with spikes.
At noon we rest for a bowl of rice, then start again.
All this so that the great Iron Horse
can travel across America in only days
unlike the months it takes by wagon or coach.

Soon our eastward-bound line will join
with the westward-bound Union Pacific Line.
Hundreds will celebrate this great human feat.

Let the others have the glory and fame.
We have earned money for our families
and respect from our bosses for a job well-done.

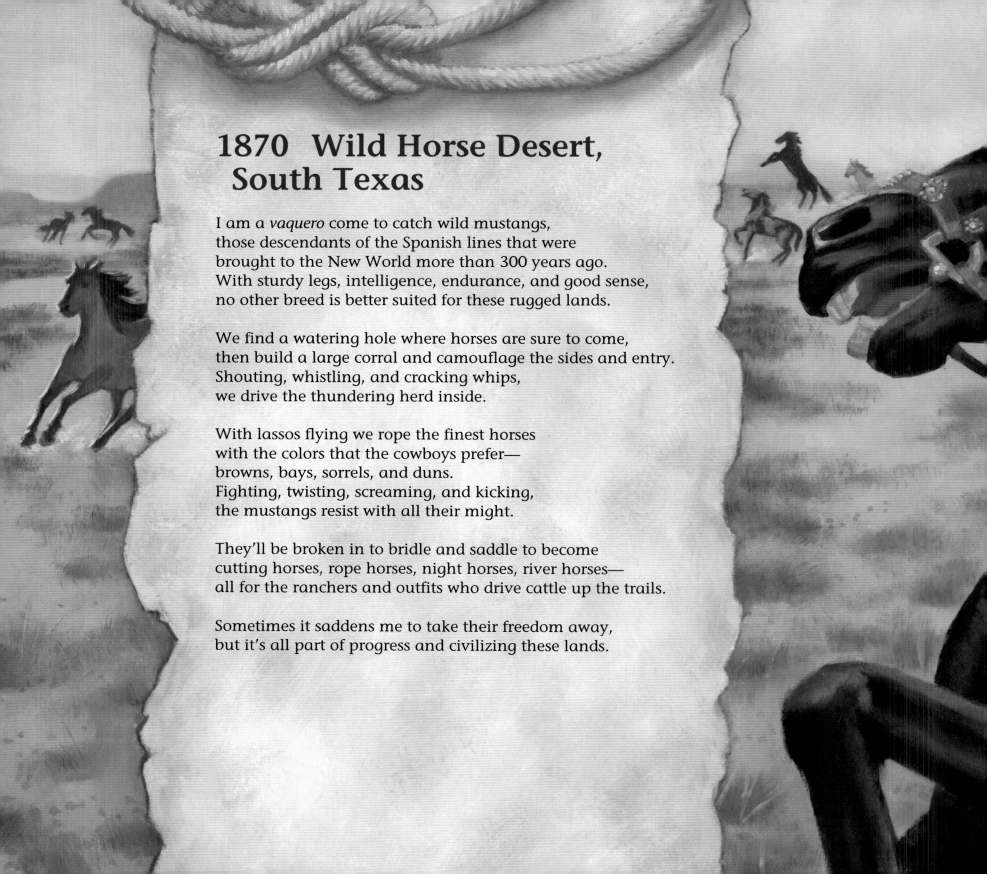

1870 Wild Horse Desert, South Texas

I am a *vaquero* come to catch wild mustangs,
those descendants of the Spanish lines that were
brought to the New World more than 300 years ago.
With sturdy legs, intelligence, endurance, and good sense,
no other breed is better suited for these rugged lands.

We find a watering hole where horses are sure to come,
then build a large corral and camouflage the sides and entry.
Shouting, whistling, and cracking whips,
we drive the thundering herd inside.

With lassos flying we rope the finest horses
with the colors that the cowboys prefer—
browns, bays, sorrels, and duns.
Fighting, twisting, screaming, and kicking,
the mustangs resist with all their might.

They'll be broken in to bridle and saddle to become
cutting horses, rope horses, night horses, river horses—
all for the ranchers and outfits who drive cattle up the trails.

Sometimes it saddens me to take their freedom away,
but it's all part of progress and civilizing these lands.

1875 Near the Red River, Indian Territory

I am a cowboy driving a bellowing herd
of lanky longhorns up the Chisholm Trail.

I've been in the saddle for three months,
through blistering heat and raging storms
that scattered the stampeding steers.

I've ridden point, swing, drag, and night herd, too.
Got bucked off more times than a hound has ticks
from the broncos in the *remuda* that aren't quite broke.
Been stung by ants and scorpions and bit by a snake;
my chaps are scratched up by cactus and scrub.

'Round the chuck wagon I've eaten Cooky's poor fixings
and drank enough thick, sugared coffee to drown a horse.

I've watched a million stars light up the sky
and heard the coyote howl at the moon.
I've told tall tales around the campfire
and slept with my saddle for a pillow.

It's a lonely life, but you won't find a happier man
than a cowboy riding up the Chisholm Trail.

1878 Great Plains

I am a lad of twelve on my first train ride
across these wild and wooly Western lands.

When I hear the boom of rifle shots far ahead,
my heart pounds with excitement and fear.
I am sure it is Jesse James pulling off a theft,
or maybe it's Comanche after our scalps.

Suddenly I see hundreds of dead buffalo
strewn over the blood-stained grass and earth.

"Buffalo hunters," a woman says in disgust.
"They will skin off the hides and cut out the tongues,
leaving the carcasses to rot in the sun—
thousands and thousands of pounds of meat."

Some escaping buffalo dash across the tracks,
but the train's cowcatcher pushes them aside.
Men on the train aim Sharps rifles out the windows
and for sport fire at the buffalo running away.

"The buffalo will soon be gone," a soldier says.
"Then maybe Indians will stay on the reservations."

As the train moves on, I slump back down.
I wish it had been Jesse James after all.

1880 Dodge City, Kansas

I am the sheriff in these parts, trying to enforce the law.
This town started as a stop on the Old Santa Fe Trail.
When the railroads arrived, the population boomed
with buffalo hunters, railroad men, soldiers,
and more saloons than you could count.

Nowadays cattle drivers come up from Texas
with herds of cows for shipment east by rail.
After months in the saddle, those cowboys let loose
with whiskey, shouting, and fighting in the street.

Now and then a shootist like Clay Allison
moseys into town stirring up trouble,
or professional gamblers have a quarrel.

I throw the worst ones in the calaboose,
and some get buried up yonder on Boot Hill.

Glad I have my Colt .45 to keep the peace.

1886 Arizona Territory

I am a Buffalo Soldier, a former slave
who joined this all-Negro regiment in 1866.

Had lots of duties over the years—building roads,
repairing forts, protecting settlers and wagon trains,
helping telegraph men and railroad surveyors.
Fought off bandits robbing stagecoach lines.

But today is a special day for the Tenth Cavalry,
because that ol' wily Apache, Geronimo,
has finally surrendered for good.

For close to thirty years, he raided and killed
with a brutal vengeance as hot as the desert sun.
He moved like a ghost in jagged sierras and canyons—
soldiers might as well have been chasing the wind.

The major says this marks the end of the Indian Wars,
for all the other great Indian leaders are dead
or living on reservations here and there.

Can't say I blame that old, thieving renegade
for fighting for his freedom for so long.

1900 New York City

I am Annie Oakley, a markswoman
who can shoot a hole in a silver dollar
or a cigarette from a gentleman's mouth.
I've been part of Buffalo Bill's Wild West since 1885.

Bill Cody is a real-life frontier hero;
he has known everything that's in his show—
from Indian attacks to stagecoach robberies,
from buffalo hunts to cowboys and scouts,
gunfighters, gamblers, and outlaws.
These eastern folk just eat it up,
and so do the dukes and lords
and queens and kings of Europe.

Times are changing as years go by—
yesterday I saw horseless carriages
chugging down Fifth Avenue.

Yes, the Western frontier is fading fast.
Soon no one will remember it at all.

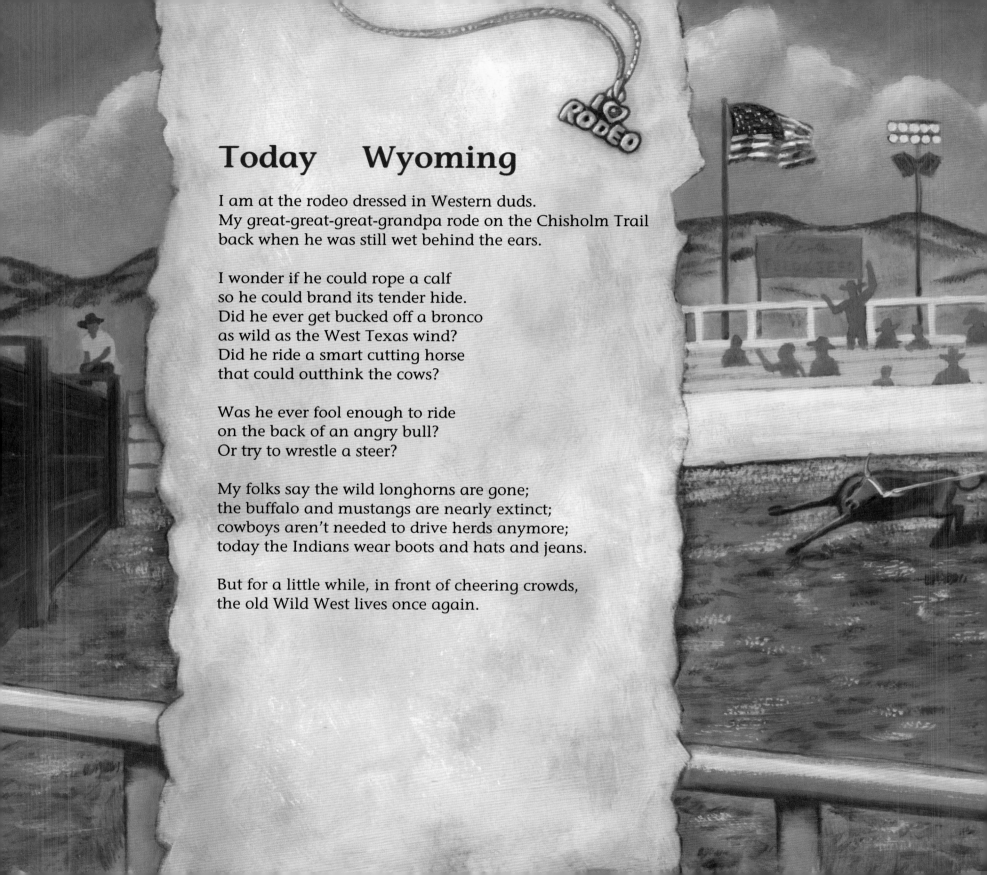

Today   Wyoming

I am at the rodeo dressed in Western duds.
My great-great-great-grandpa rode on the Chisholm Trail
back when he was still wet behind the ears.

I wonder if he could rope a calf
so he could brand its tender hide.
Did he ever get bucked off a bronco
as wild as the West Texas wind?
Did he ride a smart cutting horse
that could outthink the cows?

Was he ever fool enough to ride
on the back of an angry bull?
Or try to wrestle a steer?

My folks say the wild longhorns are gone;
the buffalo and mustangs are nearly extinct;
cowboys aren't needed to drive herds anymore;
today the Indians wear boots and hats and jeans.

But for a little while, in front of cheering crowds,
the old Wild West lives once again.

Historical Note

In 1800, the boundary of the United States stopped at the Mississippi River. On the other side, all the way to the Pacific Ocean, lay lands claimed by Spain, France, and Great Britain.

In 1803, the young United States purchased 828,000 square miles of land from France. Called the Louisiana Purchase, this area included all the lands of the headwaters that drained toward the Mississippi River.

President Thomas Jefferson convinced Congress to fund an expedition to the newly acquired lands. He placed Capt. Meriwether Lewis and 2nd Lt. William Clark in charge of the expedition called the Corps of Discovery. They were to explore and find a navigable water route from the Mississippi River to the Pacific Ocean. Lewis also collected specimens of new flora and fauna and informed Indians that the United States wanted peace and only to trade furs. Clark drew maps and charts. Both men kept journals.

In May 1804, Lewis and Clark started up the Missouri River with a keelboat and two large pirogues. That autumn, they stopped at the Mandan Villages in what is now North Dakota to build a fort and spend the winter. They hired a French trapper named Toussaint Charbonneau as a translator. His teenage Indian wife, Sacagawea, who had an infant son, spoke two native languages and was helpful in many ways.

The explorers wound their way up rivers, carrying the smaller boats around waterfalls and rapids and building dugout canoes when needed. They crossed the Rocky Mountains and, by way of the Columbia River, finally reached the Pacific Ocean in autumn of 1805. They built another fort and spent their second winter there, returning to St. Louis, Missouri, in September 1806.

They did not find a continuous water passage but saw that beaver were abundant. At this time the beaver fur trade was extremely lucrative. Since the 1550s, beaver pelts had been used to make hats. After the European beaver was trapped to near extinction, demand arose for North American beaver. The British Hudson's Bay Company experienced great success. John Jacob Astor, who founded the American Fur Company, became the first American millionaire. Not only did French-Canadian, British, and American men trap beaver, Native Americans also trapped and traded the pelts for items such as weapons, tools, and glass beads.

By the 1820s, three thousand rugged, independent Americans called mountain men were trapping beaver. As the supply of animals dwindled, the price rose so high that hat makers started using silk instead. By 1840, the fur trade in America had declined significantly. Many former mountain men, such as Kit Carson, became guides for westward expeditions, the U.S. Army, and wagon trains. In 1846, Great Britain gave up claim to the Oregon/Washington areas where otter furs were sought.

Spain had claimed the southwest region centuries earlier, in the 1500s. Catholic missions and colonies were established in New Mexico, Texas, and California. In 1821, the area called "Mexico" won its independence from Spain. In 1824, several hundred Americans received permission to colonize parts of the Mexican province called "Texas." By 1836, the English-speaking Texian population had grown to 35,000. They rebelled against Mexico and won their independence, becoming the Republic of Texas. After the United States annexed Texas in 1845, the Mexican-American War began over contested borders. Mexico lost that war and, in 1848, sold its North American lands to the United States.

The United States now extended from sea to sea. Seeing western expansion as a God-given right called Manifest Destiny, thousands of emigrants seeking cheap land launched their prairie schooners onto the Oregon Trail, which had been established in the early 1800s by fur traders. From 1846 through 1869, approximately 400,000 settlers made the 2,000-mile trip from Missouri to Oregon Country, facing tremendous hardships. Offshoots of the main trail took people to Utah, California, and Montana.

In 1848, gold was discovered in the American River near the Sierra Nevada Mountains in California. Soon "Gold Fever" spread, luring 300,000 men seeking their fortunes. Some came by boat, others by land. Boom towns such as San Francisco popped up almost overnight. Merchants became wealthy by charging high fees for tools and supplies. By 1853, most of the loose gold in the streams and rivers was gone and only mining companies with heavy equipment could retrieve gold from the mountains.

Now that the United States was one contiguous nation, communication between East and West became imperative. One of the colorful but short-lived communication enterprises was the Pony Express, which carried mail from Missouri to California in only ten days by using relay stations to change horses. When telegraphs were installed across the continent in 1861, the Pony Express ended. Stagecoach lines, such as the Overland, Butterfield, and Wells Fargo lines, continued to carry mail, passengers, and cargo.

Railroad companies saw the profit of having trains run between Missouri and California. In 1865, work crews began the tremendous task of building tracks for two railroad lines: the Central Pacific that headed east from California and the Union Pacific that traveled west. The Central Pacific labor force consisted of mostly Chinese immigrants while the Union Pacific used many Irish immigrants and former Civil War soldiers. In 1869, the two railroad tracks joined at Promontory Point, Utah. This ended the need for long stagecoach trips and wagon trains.

Although Spain had lost her North American lands, the Spanish missions and ranchers left an enduring legacy: cows and horses. Over the years, livestock escaped and multiplied until immense herds ran free. Native Americans captured horses and became skilled riders. This changed the way of life for the Plains Indians who depended on the buffalo for survival. With horses, they could now follow the herds and ensure a steady food supply.

Millions of longhorn cattle and wild horses called mustangs roamed Texas. Anyone who caught and branded a mustang or longhorn took ownership. After the Civil War, there was a meat shortage in the eastern states. Enterprising Texas cattlemen collected their branded cattle from the open range and drove them over established cattle trails that led mostly north to Kansas and Nebraska. From there the cattle were shipped east by rail. The Chisholm Trail alone handled five million cattle during its existence.

Cow towns such as Abilene, Kansas, and Dodge City, Kansas, boomed because of the cattle industry. At first these towns were lawless meccas for rowdy cowboys, gunslingers, gamblers, saloons, and houses of ill repute. Citizens hired soon-to-be-famous gunmen like Wyatt Earp, Bat Masterson, and Wild Bill Hickok to keep the law.

As time passed, other cattle breeds were favored over the legendary longhorn. That, along with the invention of barbed wire and railroads in Texas, brought the era of great cattle drives to an end. Although the period only lasted about twenty years (1866-1886), it created the myth of the American cowboy that still lives today.

The Homestead Act of 1862 allowed a person to receive free land if he or she farmed it for five years. Lands were made available in the West for people who could not otherwise afford to own land. Some emigrants settled on prairies of the Great Plains, building their houses out of sod since there were few trees. In Indian Territory (now Oklahoma) several land rushes were held. People lined up and at the firing of a cannon rushed forth to stake out a claim in the newly opened lands that had formerly belonged to Native Americans.

As more people settled the West, Native American tribes were forcibly moved to areas set aside for them called reservations. The federal government promised to take care of them, but as time passed the Indians' main source of food, the buffalo, was methodically slaughtered by buffalo hunters, first to supply railroad workers and army soldiers with meat, then later for the buffalo skins only. Almost sixty million buffalo were killed in a thirty-year period. Many Americans hoped this extinction would make the Indians stay on the reservations and become farmers and ranchers.

Instead, this policy caused resistance. Some Indian nations refused to go to the reservations or busted out of the reservations to become renegades. They reasoned that since the Americans were killing their buffalo it was fair for them to take American cattle and horses. This led to the Indian Wars—hostile encounters between Native Americans and U.S. soldiers, such as the Battle of Little Bighorn (1876), in which General Custer and all his troops were killed under the leadership of Sitting Bull and Crazy Horse. In the Southwest, leaders such as Victorio, Cochise, and Geronimo defied capture. The Massacre of Wounded Knee in 1890, during which U.S. soldiers killed men, women, and children of a renegade group, is considered the last Indian resistance.

In 1890, the U.S. Census Bureau announced that the Western frontier was closed; westward expansion was over. As the Old West vanished, dime novels with Western heroes and Wild West shows such as that of William "Buffalo Bill" Cody became immensely popular.

Today, thanks to Western novels, movies, and events like rodeos, the Wild West continues to be one of the most uniquely American aspects of U.S. history.

Glossary

Beaver hat – a hat made of felted beaver fur, for example, a top hat

Bison – another name for an American buffalo

Black Hills – a region in South Dakota and Wyoming sacred to Plains Indians

Bronco – a wild or partly-broken horse, usually a mustang

Buffalo chips – dried buffalo dung used for fuel

Calaboose – a jail

Calico – colorful cotton cloth printed in figured patterns

Chaps – leather coverings worn over the legs for protection

Chuck wagon – the cook's wagon, full of supplies for the trail drive

Colt .45 – popular pistol used in the 1800s made by Samuel Colt

Cradleboard – a structure used for carrying a baby, usually on the mother's back

Great Basin – a region in the far-western U.S. that contains desert and mountainous areas

Great Waters – another name for the Pacific Ocean

Great White Father – President of the United States; in 1806 he was Thomas Jefferson

Horseless carriage – nickname for the earliest automobiles

Iron Horse – nickname for the early steam-engine trains

Indian pony – a mustang

Indian Territory – area where Indians were relocated onto reservations; Oklahoma

Panning – swirling water and silt in a shallow pan so gold pieces will rise to the surface

Pirogue – a flat-bottomed rowboat, sometimes with a sail

Prairie schooner – a sturdy covered wagon used by pioneers

Prospector – one who searches a region for minerals or precious stones

Remuda – a string of horses used by cowboys on cattle drives

Shootist – a gunfighter, an expert marksman

Sluice – a trough through which water is run to separate gold

Tatanka [also totanka] – the Sioux word for buffalo

Tipi [also teepee] – a conical structure made out of hides

Vaquero – a cowboy of Spanish ancestry

Selected Bibliography

Barbour, Barton H. *Jedediah Smith: No Ordinary Mountain Man.* Norman, OK: University of Oklahoma Press, 2009.

Beck, Warren A. and Ynez. D. Haase. *Historical Atlas of the American West.* Norman, OK: University of Oklahoma Press, 1989

Billington, Ray Allen and Martin Ridge. *Westward Expansion: A History of the American Frontier.* Albuquerque, NM: University of New Mexico Press, 2001.

Blevins, Winfred. *Dictionary of the American West.* New York, NY: Facts on File, 1993.

Cassidy, James J. et al, eds. *Through Indian Eyes.* Pleasantville, NY: Readers Digest Association, 1995.

Cody, William F. *The Life of Buffalo Bill.* London: Studio Editions, 1994.

Hollister, C. Warren et al. *The West Transformed.* Fort Worth, TX: Harcourt College Publishers, 2000.

Johnston, Robert D. *The Making of America.* Washington, D.C.: National Geographic Society, 2002.

Levinson, Sanford and Bartholomew Sparrow, eds. *The Louisiana Purchase and American Expansion 1803-1898.* Lanham, MD. Rowan and Littlefield Publishers, 2005.

McGrath, Patrick. *The Lewis and Clark Expedition.* Morrison, NJ: Silver Burdette Co., 1985.

Meldahl, Keith Heyer. *Hard Road West: History and Geology Along the Gold Rush Trail.* Chicago: University of Chicago Press, 2007.

Miller, James and John Thompson. *Almanac of American History.* Washington, D.C.: National Geographic Society, 2006.

Stegner, Page. *Winning the Wild West: The Epic Story of the American Frontier 1800-1899.* San Diego, CA: Tehabi Books, 2002.

Books for Young Readers

Blumberg, Rhoda. *The Incredible Journey of Lewis and Clark*. New York, NY: Lothrop, Lee and Shepard Books, 1987.

Chambers, Catherine E. *Frontier Village: A Town is Born*. Mahwah, NJ: Troll Communications, 1999.

————. *Texas Roundup: Life on the Range*. Mahwah, NJ: Troll Communications, 1984.

Erickson, Paul. *Daily Life in a Covered Wagon*. New York, NY: Puffin Books, 1994.

Fletcher, Sydney E. *The Big Book of Cowboys*. New York, NY: Grosset and Dunlop, 1976.

Friedman, Mel. *The Oregon Trail*. New York, NY: Scholastic, 2013.

Harvey, Brett, illus. by Deborah Kogan Ray. *My Prairie Year: Based on the Diary of Elenore Plaisted*. New York, NY: Holiday House, 1986.

Hook, Jason, illus. by Richard Hook. *Men at Arms Series # 163: The American Plains Indians*. London: Osprey Publishing, 1991.

Jones, Evan and Dale L. Morgan, eds. *Trappers and Mountain Men*. New York, NY: American Heritage Junior Library, 1961.

Knight, Amelia Stewart, illus. by Michael McCurdy. *The Way West: Journal of a Pioneer Woman*. New York, NY: Simon & Schuster Books for Young Readers, 1993.

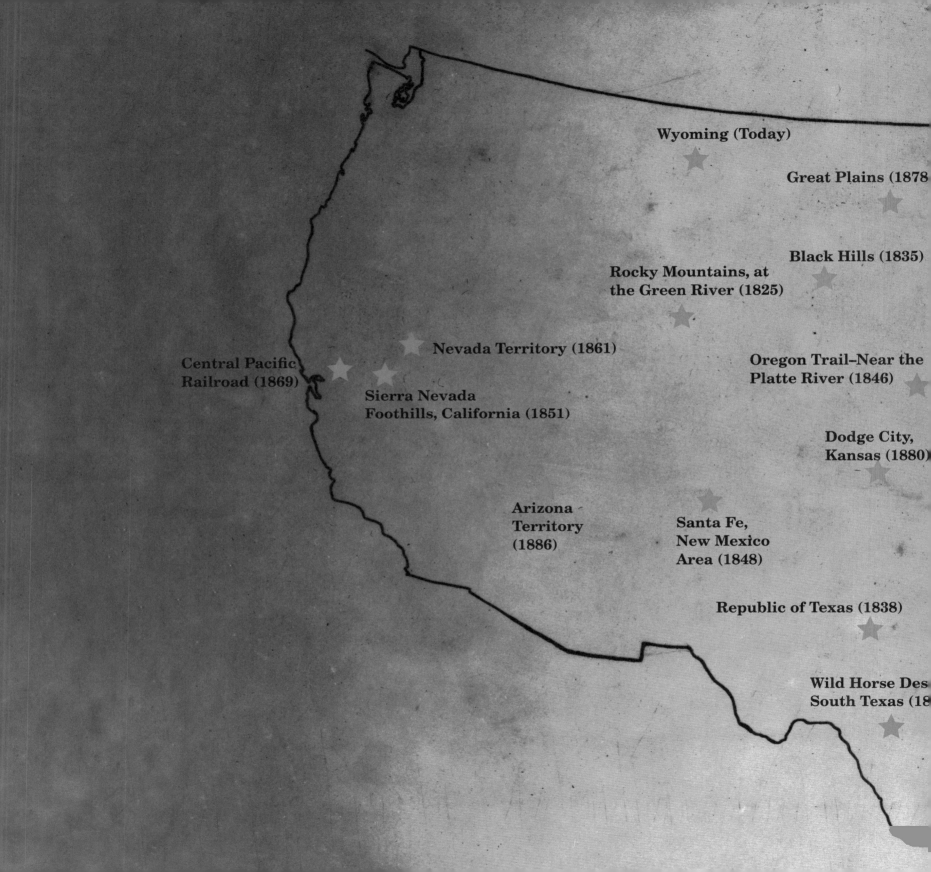

Wyoming (Today)

Great Plains (1878

Black Hills (1835)

Rocky Mountains, at
the Green River (1825)

Nevada Territory (1861)

Central Pacific
Railroad (1869)

Oregon Trail–Near the
Platte River (1846)

Sierra Nevada
Foothills, California (1851)

Dodge City,
Kansas (1880)

Arizona
Territory
(1886)

Santa Fe,
New Mexico
Area (1848)

Republic of Texas (1838)

Wild Horse Des
South Texas (18